At Home

Susan Canizares
Samantha Berger

Scholastic Inc.
New York • Toronto • London • Auckland • Sydney
Mexico City • New Delhi • Hong Kong

PlaceBook™ Notes

Can you name the one thing that you use most at home? It's probably water! You use water to wash dishes and clothes—and to wash yourself. We use 25 to 50 gallons of water just to take a five minute shower. And it takes 2 to 7 gallons of water to flush a toilet. Do you know how much water you use to brush your teeth? About 2 gallons. You also use water to cook and clean. If you help wash the dishes after dinner, you probably use almost 20 gallons! An average household uses about 107,000 gallons of water a year.

Character Design and Illustrations: James Williamson and Alex Ostroy
Book Design: James Salerno
Photo Research: Amla Sanghvi
PlaceBook Notes: Valerie Garfield

Photographs: Cover & p. 12: Andre Gallant/Image Bank; p. 3: Ariel Skelley/Stock Market; p. 4: Jalandoni/Monkmeyer; p. 5: M. Ferguson/Photo Edit; p. 6: Shackman/Monkmeyer; p. 7: Shackman/Monkmeyer; p. 8: Andrew Errington/Tony Stone; p. 9: Goodwin/Monkmeyer; p. 10: Laura Dwight/Photo Edit; p. 11: Dunn/Monkmeyer; p. 13: Jalandoni/Monkmeyer; p. 14: Bob Daemmrich/Stock Boston

Library of Congress Cataloging-in-Publication Data
Canizares, Susan 1960-
At home / Susan Canizares, Samantha Berger.
p. cm.
Summary: Photographs and simple text explore the many different things one can do at home.
ISBN 0-439-15367-0
1. Home economics--Juvenile literature. [1. Home.] I. Berger, Samantha. II. Title.
TX148 .C35 2000
640--dc21 00-020639

Printed in the U.S.A.
ISBN 0-439-15367-0

2 3 4 5 6 7 8 9 10 05 04 03

Good morning!

It's time to get dressed.

It's time to eat.

It's time to clean up.

It’s time to draw and write.

It's time to play.

It's time to put things away.

It's time to have dinner.

It's time to brush your teeth.

It's time to take a bath.

It's time to read a story.

Good night.

Nina's Word Page

dresser

stove

refrigerator

sink

bed

mirror

bookshelf

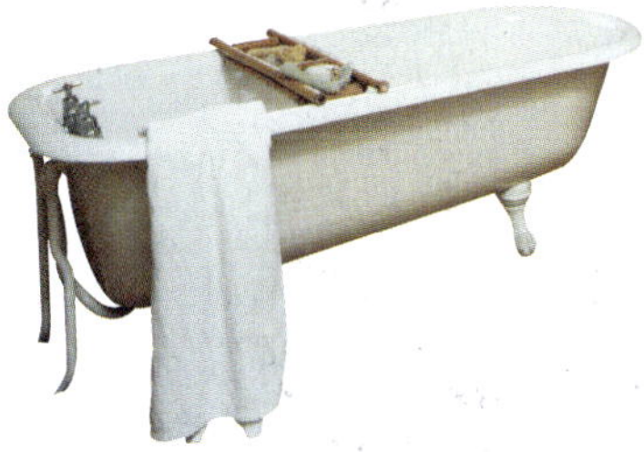

bathtub

Nina's Notes Discuss the words and pictures on this page with children. These words and pictures also appear on Nina's Word Cards 1-8. Children can use these vocabulary cards to build their own ideas about homes. Put Nina's Word Cards in a basket. Have children take turns closing their eyes and picking one card. Before the child puts the card back into the basket, ask how many of the object shown on that card can be found in his or her home. Children can also guess in which rooms of a home they might find it (bedroom, kitchen, living room). Let children name everything they can think of that can be found in one of those rooms. Have children share which room in their home is their favorite and why.

Reggie's Song Page

It's Time

Words and music by Fran Avni